MORE BEAUTIFUL

ALL-AMERICAN DECORATION

Rizzoli
NEW YORK

New York · Paris · London · Milan

MORE BEAUTIFUL

ALL-AMERICAN DECORATION

MARK D. SIKES

PHOTOGRAPHY BY AMY NEUNSINGER
TEXT BY KATHRYN O'SHEA-EVANS

TO MOM AND DAD,
DONNA AND RALPH SIKES,
THANKS FOR TEACHING ME THAT
BEAUTY IS EVERYWHERE

CONTENTS

INTRODUCTION
BEAUTY IS EVERYWHERE 10

TRADITIONAL
BRIGHT COLORS AND SOUTHERN CHARMS 40

COASTAL
BLUE AND WHITE FOREVER 80

COUNTRY
FROM RUSTIC TO MODERN 122

MEDITERRANEAN
ADVENTURE AT HOME 172

BEAUTIFUL
LIVING WITH WHAT YOU LOVE 226

RESOURCES 268
ACKNOWLEDGMENTS 271
CREDITS 272

INTRODUCTION

BEAUTY IS EVERYWHERE

No matter where you look, beauty is everywhere. It manifests itself in the simplest things: A smile. A neatly made bed. Dahlias popping like fireworks in the late summer. Ivory embroidered curtains dancing unfettered in the breeze.

I learned that important lesson growing up in the South and the Midwest, the son of a preacher and a preacher's wife. Both of my parents appreciate pretty things and fostered that interest in me early on. I remember going to the drugstore with my mother and heading straight for the magazine aisle, soaking up everything from *Vogue* to *House & Garden*. It was the start of a lifelong obsession with beauty.

When I published my first book, *Beautiful*, four years ago, I wanted to create something timeless that brought to life all of my favorite things. I decided to call this new book *More Beautiful* because it's a continuation of all I love. Take the home on these pages, which embodies my favorites: blue-and-white Portuguese tiles, a myriad of antiques, masses of wicker, stripes, checks, embroidery, and an abundance of details. It nods to style icons, *(continued on page 31)*

PREVIOUS PAGE: A Mediterranean entry is as eternally pretty as an olive tree. ABOVE: A bone-inlaid Anglo-Indian side table makes for an evocative welcome in a Provençal California entryway. OPPOSITE: The turned-wood legs of an antique Italian demilune table supply timeless appeal—prime placement for a collection of antique blue-and-white ceramics. The background fabric is Bujosa's Cabas pattern in a soft blue-green. FOLLOWING PAGES: Hanging the living room's hand-embroidered custom curtains sky-high draws the eye up into the lofty space.

Iksel's Canton Reverie scenic wallpaper, designed in the eighteenth century by the East India Company, is just as enchanting today.

We upholstered the dining room in three Brunschwig & Fils textiles—a nod to maximalist designer Renzo Mongiardino.

The client's own Delft collection lines the walls; a natural-fiber abaca rug and Provençal rush host and hostess chairs bring the room down to earth.

Calacatta marble counters, plaster pendant lights custom painted the same creamy hue as the cabinets, and a blue-and-white Portuguese tile backsplash turn a simple white kitchen into a Provençal escape.

Blue-and-white Portuguese tiles
surround French doors.
Diminutive blue-and-white tiles
are embedded in the terra-cotta.

The blue and white-striped Schumacher fabric dotting the room, a striped dhurrie, and an abundance of wicker—plus a towering potted ficus tree—brings the outdoor experience indoors. The sisal rug supplies added texture underfoot.

ABOVE: There's something in the mix that's super wonderful. Here, African ceramics and an Anglo-Indian tray sit atop an antique French table. OPPOSITE: Combined in one sitting area, African vases, a black-and-white photograph, and a wicker sofa with worn-in pillows upholstered in a Schumacher stripe evoke the south of France.

A flurry of layered antique pillows in a range of blues, with embroidered florals and vintage textiles.

Custom-painted frames in the same blue hue as the bed allow botanical prints to pop. It's a tailored ode to nature's wild grace.

too—like the way we paneled the whole dining room in fabric, which is very Renzo Mongiardino in feel.

Mongiardino's bohemian slant has always inspired me, but he's not the only one. I often look to Bill Blass, a fashion designer with classic homes and Midwestern roots; Mark Hampton, whose taste ran so unflappably all-American and refined; Oscar de la Renta, whose cane furniture and unbuttoned, neutrals-infused Dominican compounds still thrill me today; Marella Agnelli, who exemplified elegance and grace so perfectly that Richard Avedon called her "the swan"; and Jackie Kennedy, who clearly could do no wrong! These legends compel me with their impeccable style. Their timelessness is my goal, because their beauty never fades.

More Beautiful is organized by iconic home style. The "Traditional" chapter is everything the word conjures—color and wallpapers, trims galore, antiques, hand-painted objets, and both stained and painted wood pieces. "Coastal" takes its cues from the water and has a cleanliness to it: sun-faded linen and neutrals, whether you're in Newport or Malibu. "Country" is inspired by the outdoors and has a natural rusticity and ease that comes with that way of life, all distressed finishes and aged patinas. "Mediterranean"—with its copious tiles and terra-cotta and wrought iron and embroideries and paisleys—is the one I'm probably most at home with.

The last chapter, "Beautiful," is on my own house in the Hollywood Hills, which I share with my partner, Michael, and our French bulldog, Lily. While some people may think that worshipping beauty is superficial, the reality is that it's anything but: it can fortify our spirits. I often find that feeling in nature; there is something very pure and spiritual about it. What's prettier than seeing limitless blue skies as a backdrop to lush trees flourishing along a rushing brook? It's an exquisite sensory overload that doesn't cost anything, and yet it can restore anyone. The same goes at home. When you celebrate the little things more often and surround yourself with what you truly adore, you'll find that your whole world becomes infinitely more beautiful.

OPPOSITE: Here, the grasscloth wallpaper was hand-painted with stripes, adding to the room's touches of natural fibers and textures, including leather. The simple palette of neutrals, warm whites, and cerused woods provides a charming backdrop for conversation; the background fabric is Montecito Medallion by Schumacher in Neutral. FOLLOWING PAGES: Arranging two mirrorlike sitting areas back-to-back is ideal for parties—it turns an expansive living area into a cozy, welcoming respite.

In this bedroom, the mix of many Mark D. Sikes for Schumacher paisley fabrics along with ivory embroidered linens creates a warm sanctuary. Placing a tufted settee at the foot of a bed creates ample space to lounge.

PICASSO
THE LINE

Ornate touches, like a hand-embroidered headboard by Holland & Sherry, bone-inlaid boxes, and antique pottery on the mantel, give a layered, collected sensibility.

"Beauty is the
mystery of life.
It is not in
the eye, it is
in the mind."

—*Agnes Martin*

CLOCKWISE FROM TOP LEFT: Cabinets with sheer fabric add
warmth while keeping visual clutter out of sight. Wicker
from Soane Britain provides instant texture. Sunlit
soaking tubs are even more spa-like. A woven wicker
armrest feels inherently relaxing to the touch, like picking
up a straw beach bag. An overstuffed armchair
you want to sink into. Subtle patterns bewitch the eye.

TRADITIONAL
BRIGHT COLORS AND SOUTHERN CHARMS

Anyone who has ventured below the Mason-Dixon line knows that the expression "Southern charm" is doubly true when it comes to interiors. In this storied region, traditionalism reigns. The design is as tailored and classic as society blonde C. Z. Guest in a white romper at Villa Artemis, her Palm Beach estate. It can also be layered and over-the-top in the best possible way, like the homes of decorating luminary Mario Buatta—the "Prince of Chintz"—who made maximalism a must.

In the South, saturated color is celebrated: Tawny yellows. Slipper pinks. Chartreuse greens. Robin's-egg blues. They may seem as sweet as pastel candy, but they're anything but saccharine.

I fell for traditional style during my early years in Nashville. We lived in a home adorned in damask wallpaper, where the dining room was lined in mirrors and had a crystal chandelier. In traditional style, custom details are all but required, yet they must be as elegant as a Southern belle heading *(continued on page 52)*

PREVIOUS PAGE: You can never have too many trees; they're often the soul of the landscape. ABOVE: A pea-gravel walkway edged in boxwood is endlessly charming alfresco. OPPOSITE: The beauty is in the details in this traditional Montecito, California, home, where thoughtful additions like piped upholstery, chintz, and fringed sofas can beguile for decades to come. The background fabric, seen on the armchair and throw pillow, is Lee Jofa's Althea Linen in Citron. FOLLOWING PAGES: A collection of Delft plates and plenty of blues and greens draw the eye seamlessly out into the cutting gardens beyond the window. PAGES 48-49: Cane French bistro chairs at the dining table nod to Parisian cafés in the kitchen. The painting is by Ellsworth Kelly.

Collections can work wonders at highlighting architectural details, such as this sculptural fireplace mantel.

Gracious reading areas welcome moments of repose. Copious fringed and tasseled throw pillows cozy up a sitting area, inviting conversation to linger.

Painted furniture and a bamboo side chair, desk, and bench have timeless appeal that always works.

Alongside abundant greenery, layers of ikats, embroidered linens, florals, and checks give this bedroom all the layered loveliness of the garden.

to church in her Sunday dress: odes to favorite antiques, patterned wallpaper, hand-painted chinoiserie, and curated accessories and trims, culled together to form a place that's unmistakably yours. Monograms are big in the South for the same reason; it's all about personalization and developing your own aesthetic.

Nearly every traditional room I design has what I call a "hero" fabric—say, a Brunschwig & Fils floral—that may be used on the sofa and an adjacent chair alongside solids, smaller-scale prints, and vintage textiles reborn anew as throw pillows. Or occasionally I'll go maximal and apply the hero fabric on literally everything—the drapes, the walls, the furniture. Picking a pattern that's sprinkled throughout (or on everything!) sets the tone. Then all the other elements in the room become the supporting cast.

Traditional interiors also often feature collections, from Delft plates to nineteenth-century Rose Medallion china, that prove that more really *is* merrier (and more impactful, especially when placed together to form a focal point). Furniture in these spaces tends to be a mix of stained and painted wood, much of it connoting an aura of history. Modern art allows necessary breathing room and prevents all that prettiness from reading as treacly. Lush and leafy plants—whether Boston ferns or potted flowers, or even an expanse of verdant cutting gardens and centuries-old oak trees beyond the windows—also give the eye a break.

Above all, a traditional interior should feel like it's been there forever, such as Nashville's 1932 Beaux Arts–inspired Cheekwood Estate, or Swan House in Atlanta, where an Italian Mannerist facade is echoed by elaborate chinoiserie-stocked interiors. You want these spaces to feel old and chock-full of heirlooms and things passed down from one generation to the next. An inherent part of the traditional mentality is that you don't get rid of things from family—you use them, creating interiors that put not only the pretty items but also the important, sentimental things on center stage. Say it with me: more is more is *more*.

OPPOSITE: Set on pedestals, lush potted ferns bring in the outdoors in an unmissable way. A settee upholstered in a Brunschwig & Fils fabric pops against a graphic Quadrille wallcovering. FOLLOWING PAGES: A geometric abaca rug evokes a painted floor and creates a serene neutral base for patterns and colors galore.

Rose Medallion and Imari antique porcelain bring all the colors of the room together in one storied accessory.

A hand-painted Gracie
wallcovering and majolica
dishes lighten up an antique
wood hutch, adding whimsy.
Potted plants from the garden
take a formal room and
make it feel very lived in.

Displaying personal collections is a hallmark of a traditional home.

Dark mahogany furniture is a staple in Southern homes, where pieces live on for generations in the family. Here a spring garden palette enlivens antique pieces.

A hammered-brass bar sink will charm for decades.

Architect James B. Laughlin melded the original cabinetry with new updates in this 1950s Alabama kitchen, freshened up with Farrow & Ball's Parma Gray paint.

Archival prints, like fabrics from Sister Parish and Madeleine Castaing, will always be iconic.

The traditional garden room gets a fresh update with painted green wicker, white flooring, modern art, and an upholstered Parsons table.

Symmetry creates tranquility in the master bedroom, especially in a palette of blues, warm whites, and neutrals. Scalloped detailing on the upholstered four-poster bed designed by Mr. and Mrs. Bungalow for Highland House invites the eye up to travel the skyline of the room.

Botanical
fabrics and
prints pop
when paired
with
classically
tailored
stripes.

This chest of drawers
was custom painted to
match the room's fabrics.

"Youth is happy because it has the capacity to see beauty. Anyone who keeps the ability to see beauty never grows old."

Franz Kafka

A trio of antique hall chairs provide storied perches for books and myrtle topiaries in the den. The background fabric is Michael Smith's Jasper Malmaison in Fontaine.

A wallpaper from Sister Parish adorns the ceiling of the den, adding to the cozy feeling of layers upon layers of patterns, fabrics, and upholstery. A leather armchair, a streamlined lacquered coffee table, and ebonized accessories prevent the room from reading as too sweet.

Skirted tables, porcelain birds and flowers, and stacks of books are old-world ways to bring beauty into a traditional interior.

A wicker table lamp from Soane Britain mirrors the texture of hanging market baskets.

Walls lined in a Quadrille floral fabric juxtapose nicely with modern ikats, paisleys, and Indian coverlets.

A palette of corals, pinks, and watermelons provides the warmest possible welcome in a guest room. Scallop-edged D. Porthault linens, a bone-inlaid chest, and an Indian flower rug inject playfulness.

COASTAL
BLUE AND WHITE FOREVER

There is a reason vacations by the sea are so addictive. Nothing is so instantly restorative as those endless expanses of uninterrupted seafoam blues and sandy neutrals. At the coast, life's stresses ebb away, leaving room only for the essence of our days: Water. Breath. Light.

When we go to St. Barths, I find myself captivated looking out on the range of blues in the water and the way the sunlight hits the waves. It's magnificent and magical, proof that sometimes the simplest things are the most beautiful. At the beach, palette and textures and senses work together to inspire. You can achieve the same feel inside a home.

The cleanliness and graphicness one feels strolling Easton's Beach in Newport in the off-season, or East Hampton's Two Mile Hollow, or Malibu's Point Dume can be brought indoors with a calming, barefoot sensibility. I want coastal design to exude that carefree look Lauren Hutton cultivated in 1968 on the beach in Zihuatanejo, Mexico, resplendent in her sun hat and little else. That sense of seaside casualness comes into the design through midcentury-modern lines and open-plan living, which keep the look as *(continued on page 90)*

PREVIOUS PAGE: A pair of sliding barn doors are as fresh as the surf when painted glossy blue. ABOVE: Cobalt blue has the deep, dreamy quality of twilight over the sand. OPPOSITE: A graphic blue-and-white Farrow & Ball wallcovering conceals a door and turns a bleach-white spiral staircase into a moment of sculpture. The background fabric is Raoul Textiles' Poleng in Delft.

Matchstick tortoise blinds, wicker furniture, and ample baskets lend a casualness by the shore.

"Everybody needs beauty as well as bread, places to play in and pray in, where nature may heal and give strength to body and soul."

John Muir

Blue stripes in wide repeats call to mind poolside cabanas. Set against shiplap white walls, well-worn surfboards become a talking point. Exposed rafters and sky-high ceilings have the airy feel of a walk on the beach.

Slim vertical stripes in the butler's pantry turn it into a jewel of a room.

Ebonized rush barstools with bobbin details help add texture to the color blocked kitchen.

Traces of black and cobalt blues supply instant cool.

streamlined as the ocean's horizon. Weathered rattans and bamboos supply intermittent texture to each room, much like seashells dotting the sand.

Of course, the palette takes its cues from the shore—cumulus-cloud white, sea-foam blue, and the soft macaroon hue of sand—but it's more than that. The jolt of black, seen in lighting fixtures or furniture, calls to mind a cormorant flying across the water, adding punctuation to the room with its darkness. Stripes, whether on wallpaper or rugs underfoot, nod to seafaring professions and the *marinière* shirts of the French navy. Just by looking at the rooms in this chapter, you can perceive what the homeowners might wear: a white bikini, a chambray shirt, Birkenstocks, a towel. There's an inherent ease and openness to all of it. It is a bit like Babe Paley's onetime cottage (now owned by Ralph Lauren) at Round Hill, Jamaica: all exposed beams, white slipcovers, bamboo furniture, and shutters flung open to the sultry, tropically scented winds.

A coastal home doesn't need to be near a body of water (indeed, one home in this chapter is many miles inland from the ocean, in the Hollywood Hills). Coastal style is not just about what it looks like, but what it feels like. It is a relaxed way of living, with hurricane votives twinkling, breezes gently flowing, and barefoot wanderings through rooms where baskets act as nonplussed catchalls for straw hats and well-worn sandals. It is about being proudly on "island time" the moment you get home—even, or especially, if you're only minutes from the office. When you live your days in rooms like these, life really is a beach.

OPPOSITE: A paisley wallpaper by Quadrille, a spindle bed, and a skirted table let a twelve-by-twelve-foot guest room in Newport, Rhode Island, live large. The background fabric, seen on the table skirt, is Quadrille's New Batik in French Blue Navy on Tint. FOLLOWING PAGES: A note of shellwork is all but required in a coastal home, such as the mirror above the chest of drawers in this guest room. PAGES 94-95: Hurricanes, modern art, and indigo and linen textiles say "Relax."

The placement of botanical prints and use of lattice wallpaper on both ceiling and walls accentuate the roofline in a girl's room.

AGNES MARTIN

Philip Jodidio   Meier   TASCHEN

VICTORIA HAGAN   INTERIOR PORTRAITS

Texture is key, such as the hand-thrown pottery, vintage batiks, embroideries, and rope chairs in this room.

Painting all the walls in a soft, warm white provides a hushed, happy envelope for coastal living.

AGNES MARTIN

HENRI MATISSE The Cut-Outs

Richard Meier & Partners

Ultramarine blue and jutes are as natural a pairing as sea and sand.

Layering windows with relaxed Roman shades smooths their hard angles, emitting a carefree vibe.

OPPOSITE: Cerused woods are an ode to sand between one's toes.
ABOVE: In a master bedroom, English roll-arm chairs and abundant curtains juxtapose the strict lines of a wrought iron bed.

This collection of earthy, imperfect pottery summons the untamable nature of sea cliffs.

"To love beauty is to see light."

Victor Hugo

Sisal rugs add beachy texture underfoot and provide a natural base for a sculptural side table. The background fabric is Carolina Irving Textiles' Aegean Stripe in Sea/Indigo.

A faux-bois wall that looks like found driftwood tempers modern art and fixtures in a sunlit hallway. Any nook can become a reading or respite area—just add snug chairs and a table for resting a cappuccino.

Woven seating and worn woods recall seaworthy catamarans.

Cherry-picked books, dark stones, and art by Catherine Booker Jones supply a necessary edge.

OPPOSITE AND ABOVE: Stripes, stripes, and more stripes can work together handily, especially in a palette of serene neutrals. Here, a pinstripe wallcovering emphasizes architectural alcoves. FOLLOWING PAGES: Line-drawing portraits and a mix of midcentury rattan and wood furniture and accessories add to a leisurely feel.

ABOVE: An eclectic mix of art is especially pronounced thanks to the dark walls in this sitting area. OPPOSITE: A washed-linen sectional sofa beckons all the more thanks to bountiful throw pillows. A swing-arm reading light adds function and mood.

Different stripes in the same
calming blue-and-white
palette were used throughout
this dining room on the seat
cushions, rug, curtain,
and even the coved ceiling.

ABOVE AND OPPOSITE: A former garage becomes the ultimate poolhouse, thanks to a soaring open-beam ceiling and clean-lined interiors in tranquil blues, whites, and neutral textures. Swung wide, barn doors allow for quintessential (and effortless) indoor-outdoor living.

Blue and white stripes by the dozen impart a carefree air, especially amid crisp white floors and walls.

Woven finishes throughout have the cheerful, soothing sensibility of a waterfront hammock.

COUNTRY
FROM RUSTIC TO MODERN

Time in nature is essential for deep breaths and resets. It helps that visits to the countryside are inevitably back-to-basics affairs, whether you are tromping through the leafy vineyards of Napa or the centuries-old fields of a Virginia horse farm. Perfectionism fades away, and the energizing wild of the outdoors is championed in its place.

If you have ever been to Napa, you know how reinvigorating it can be. The landscape is absolutely unbelievable: the symmetry of the rolling vineyards is captivating, the colors so inspiring. There is a feeling when you're there; it's casual, comfortable, and inviting, but it's also ineffably cool.

To bring that sensation indoors in a country-style home, I often begin with a Napa-inspired palette: verdant olive greens, chestnuts, caramels, and touches of lilac that appear to burst before a foundation of sky blue and grass green. They're the same hues you see in a cabernet sauvignon vineyard, with their tidy parallel rows stretching to the horizon. Set against *(continued on page 132)*

PREVIOUS PAGE: Hedges of Carolina cherry laurel hem this shingled house in history. These particular gardens were designed by Janell Hobart of Denler Hobart Gardens. OPPOSITE: A Portola Valley, California, home designed by Walker Warner Architects. The entryway feels especially large thanks to a narrow bench and streamlined artwork by Caio Fonseca. ABOVE: Outdoor living spaces beckon year-round when they're fitted with all the trappings of indoor spaces, including plenty of lighting and comfortable seating. The background fabric is Peter Dunham Textiles' Isfahan Stripe in Blue/Green. FOLLOWING PAGES: An arbor shrouded in climbing garden roses.

Black is like punctuation in a room. Sparingly used rustic touches—such as reclaimed woods, weathered stone, and unpretentious pottery—are all but required in country homes.

neutral walls and sisal rugs underfoot, with touches of Carolina and cornflower blues, these rooms evoke fresh air. Key finishes—such as shingles, iron fixtures, zinc, and reclaimed wood—set a pastoral tone.

The first house in this chapter is near Portola Valley, California, and has an amazing vegetable cutting garden that inspired the interior. The second is in Napa, and the palette comes directly from surrounding wineries: there, you have more lilacs—a reference to the region's bountiful grapes—and beautiful, warm ranges of color mixed with green.

I often select furniture that is slightly patinaed, like a bobbin chair where the polish is worn off a bit from years of use. Layers of Swedish antiques mixed with modern elements make these rooms feel comfortable, cozy, and collected over time. Simplified walls in delicate palettes put a spotlight on modern-art collections and hand-hewn, earthy pottery. I will employ my trademark blue and white stripes, but you'll notice they're typically much wider in a country house, seen in simple hand-hooked cotton rugs and stair runners with homespun, whip-stitched edges. It's all a subtle reference to bucolic hills and the undulating nature of the vineyard landscape.

Above all, in the country, there is a sense that imperfection *is* perfection. These are homes where you may spy a hint of dirt on the mudroom floor or cut stems wilting gracefully in the flower room. It's a lifestyle: both of these clients really use the vegetables they glean from their plantings—they even can them! Every room you see here is meant to be used and actually is, which only adds to the homes' evocative charm. They're beautiful the way a gentleman's farm is beautiful: carefully tended and yet untamable by design.

PREVIOUS PAGES: The warm tones in a muted antique carpet and neutral-on-neutral patterns echo the light in this sun-drenched living room. OPPOSITE: A bounty of neutrals and chestnuts combine for an earthy look, just like the landscape beyond the windows. The modern art piece ties each hue in the sitting area together.

ABOVE: A range of greens form a natural accompaniment to blues and flax hues, thanks to the colors culled from the gardens outside. OPPOSITE: A banquette maximizes space in a breakfast area and has the added bonus of under-seat storage.

Hues of flax, olive green, and denim blue exude an organic feel in a country home, even in ornate patterns. In gleaming white, a collection of hand-hewn pottery from Hudson Grace feels fresh.

A soapstone sink seems age-old in the mudroom. It's an idyllic place for cutting flowers.

Letting flower bushes and hedges overgrow a bit imparts a wild aura that satisfies the soul.

A butcher-block island, matchstick bamboo blinds, and striped dhurries forge a warm welcome in the otherwise white-on-white kitchen. An outsize papier-mâché lamp casts a soft glow over the island and turns it into an unmissable focal point.

ABOVE: A platform bed in a guest room allows for bountiful basket storage underneath. Windows on three of the four walls provide an eagle's-eye view over the lush gardens below. OPPOSITE: Fresh hydrangea cuttings ensure guests awake to a farm-fresh moment of beauty. The background fabric is Lisa Fine Textiles' Lahore linen in Peacock.

A green Rose Tarlow Melrose House lamp matches the verdant hues beyond the windows in a hallway.

Walls in Farrow & Ball's Pale Powder are a dreamlike backdrop for a palette of seafoams and whites.

ABOVE: A custom chandelier with an antiqued iron finish sets a storied tone in this lanai that peeps out on the grounds and Portola Valley beyond. Wicker chairs bring the outdoors in. OPPOSITE: Shingled walls, antique wooden bowls, and a vintage metal industrial credenza make the indoors feel decidedly outdoorsy.

"Everything has beauty,
but not everyone sees it."

Confucius

Deep moody blues, detailed floor tiles, and dark wood furniture can
give an interior the feeling that it's been there for decades. The background fabric is Soane Britain's Dianthus Chintz in Lapis on Ivory Linen.

When you limit your color
palette to hues found in
surrounding nature—such as
the blues, greens, lilacs,
aubergines, and deep
chestnuts that evoke the
vineyards of Napa—you can
go wild with multiple patterns
without overwhelming. Using
well-worn wood furniture
pieces, such as a Gustavian
chair, is a classic country look.

The colors of the vineyard inspired a beautiful menagerie of subtle small prints and patterns.

There's little more merry than a leaf green sofa with cornflower blue piping. Repeating the colors throughout the space helps draw attention to those little yet impactful details.

OPPOSITE: The natural woven fibers on the chandelier and chairs nod to the plantings outside. ABOVE: Bronze, brushed brass, and stainless accents on a La Cornue stove, range hood, and over-island pendants provide a centuries-old look in the kitchen.

A long farmhouse table lined in simple Shaker-inspired chairs and bountiful soft linen curtains cozy up an indoor-outdoor room with soaring ceilings. The sitting area by the stone fireplace provides a warm perch for taking in the rolling vineyards beyond the bronze patio doors.

An intimate sitting area gives a great room a snug feel. Hardwearing indoor-outdoor fabrics mean nothing's too precious for use.

"Love of beauty
is taste. The
creation of
beauty is art."

Ralph Waldo Emerson

CLOCKWISE FROM TOP LEFT: A collection of antique
canes ready for a country stroll. A Christopher Farr
Cloth botanic wallcovering is downright cheeky
when it overtakes a powder room. A country lifestyle
must: a basket of shoes by the entry for easy
comings and goings. An antique rattan table. An
Ellsworth Kelly artwork pops in a countrified setting.
Diminutive floor tiles charm all the more. FOLLOWING
PAGES: Copious stripes, geometrics, and scallops will
snug up any bedroom (these two are separated by
a Jack-and-Jill bathroom, shown in the foreground).

YOU MAY LIKE

AGNES MARTIN

Fabrics by Sister Parish, D. Porthault bed linens, and geometric block prints are fun in lilacs, greens, and blues. A Swedish console and midcentury-inspired floor and table lamps impart an eclectic note.

"Wisdom is the abstract of
the past, but beauty is
the promise of the future."

Oliver Wendell Holmes

A wallcovering by Sister Parish becomes all the more alluring in a guest
room when it also graces the proverbial "fifth wall": the ceiling. Guests of
all ages will delight in sleeping in slipcovered antique twin beds.

In an attic, slanted ceilings become an architectural asset when sheathed in a Soane Britain floral wallcovering. The addition of plenty of other patterns, including country checks, florals, and striped rugs, only adds to the charm. As you know, blue loves green.

Wide green stripes modernize and visually widen a pristine white rec room.

Rattans and greens say "alfresco picnic" at a glance, all year round.

A soaring white shiplap ceiling, garden greens and natural wood, and touches of midcentury rattan give the rec room's sitting area the unmistakably fresh feeling of just-cut grass. Setting multiple side tables at varying heights ensures everyone has a spot to place his or her glass of wine.

MEDITERRANEAN

ADVENTURE AT HOME

Not long after Italian socialite and style icon Marella Agnelli lost her husband, she fell for another love: Aïn Kassimou, a thirty-acre estate in Marrakech. Erected in the late 1800s for Olga Tolstoy and later owned by the Hermès family, it became a pleasure project for Agnelli, who transformed its gardens into manicured retreats abundant with pool pavilions, fountains, trailing bougainvillea, and a lake dotted with water lilies. As she wrote, "One is never really 'done' with a garden, just as one is never 'done' with life. Day by day and step by step, one just keeps on finding new and clever ways to make them flourish, both in sunshine and in storm."

Enchanting people is often easier to do in Morocco. In fact, the entire region around the Mediterranean Sea—from Marrakech to the island of Majorca, Spain—has created design aesthetics that are some of my favorites for that very reason. Both Mediterranean and its sister style, Moroccan, cast a spell that can transport you. Part of that is the mainstays of the color palette: reds, corals, neutrals, and blues, all providing a warm yet unexpected welcome. *(continued on page 209)*

PREVIOUS PAGE: Details delight in the open air. ABOVE: Ornate details in this Mediterrannean house are meant to conjure the feeling of faraway lands. OPPOSITE: Terra-cotta tiles, a Moorish mirror, and an antique Italian console do wonders to achieve the effect in an instant. The background fabric is Brunschwig & Fils Menars Border II in Spice. FOLLOWING PAGES: Bone-inlaid Anglo-Indian antiques echo the elaborate coffered ceiling of this alfresco sitting area inspired by Morocco's indoor-outdoor gardens. The ceiling is a hand-painted antique from Italy.

"A thing of beauty is a joy for ever."

—*John Keats*

CLOCKWISE FROM TOP LEFT: Things are always looking up—literally, when your antique Italian coffered ceilings are adorned with hand-painted panels. Moroccan blue-and-white plates. Colorful Moroccan tiles can make for magic underfoot. A Moroccan sconce casts a bewitching glow after dark. A menagerie of intricately patterned pillows in ikats, paisleys, and more. Orchids bring exoticism with them wherever they roam. FOLLOWING PAGES: Imposing palms bring literal life to the living room, their liveliness reflected in a bone-inlaid Moroccan mirror.

A modern art piece contrasts beautifully with an antique French sideboard.

Layering antique rugs over a woven abaca rug has all the seduction of a Bedouin tent in any interior.

Bielecky Brothers wicker chairs, a Pierre Frey fabric, woven side chairs—texture makes perfect.

Blue-and-white tiles are legendary in the Mediterranean region; here, Portuguese tiles line the stair risers at right and even the wall.

RIGHT: Given the chance to fling open French doors to a gurgling fountain, do it—especially if you'd like to invoke the simple pleasures of a Moroccan riad. The handmade surface of plaster walls is a trademark of Mediterranean style. FOLLOWING PAGES: Saturated blues, neutrals, and a custom wood bar designed by architect Paul Brant Williger emit an antique aura in the sitting room.

Ebonized woods visually
unite this sitting area, where
masculine and feminine
elements combine. Wrought
iron touches throughout
exude old-world timeless-
ness, and a vase of tall
blooming branches
brings a note of undomesti-
cated nature indoors.

A blue-and-white Portuguese tile backsplash and brass touches warm up a kitchen with a soaring open-beam ceiling. Glass-fronted cabinets put eye-catching china on display.

A functional corner banquette has the welcoming factor of a café, but when swathed in multiple fabrics—block prints here, French ticking stripes there—it feels more like a farmhouse in southern Spain.

Blue and white-striped lounge chairs conjure the beaches of Ibiza, Spain, and echo the hues of the pool and sky above.

Mediterranean blue trim is eye candy outdoors, especially under California skies.

"Beauty is being the best possible version of yourself, inside and out."

Audrey Hepburn

An exquisite shellwork
mirror by Atelier MVM
in Los Angeles.

Period furniture, such as
an English desk and Anglo-
Indian chair with
intricate spindled legs,
becomes even more
sculptural against a light
blue-and-ivory color
scheme. The bedside
table is cozied up in a rich
paisley wool skirt.

Moroccan tiles in blue and white adorn the floors of this bathroom.

Brass finishings and marble, shown here in the fixtures and tub, have been used since the days of ancient man. No wonder they read as endlessly appealing.

ABOVE: Nothing says old-world Europe like tapestries, tile, and a claw-footed Italian commode. OPPOSITE: Pairing a leather-upholstered settee and slipcovered Italian chairs creates a nice contrast in a hall with terra-cotta floors. FOLLOWING PAGES: Arranging multiple sitting areas ensures there's plenty of room for everyone to put their feet up. The artwork is by Kit Reuther.

"I hate pretty. It's a very empty word. It gives a bad name to beauty."

— Oscar de la Renta

I love the Mediterranean style's plaster walls and terra-cotta floors, and of course all the blue-and-white Portuguese tiles. The ornate patterns of batiks, suzanis, paisleys, and even Anglo-Indian bone-inlaid furniture all come together in a cinematic way that can evoke faraway lands, even when they're stateside. I will often balance their allure with soft leathers, simple dhurries, deep mahogany Italian furniture, and the strictness of iron railings and lighting fixtures. In rooms like these, you can imagine bohemian glamazon Talitha Getty in repose, wearing her vivid caftan and white harem pants.

In Southern California, Spanish Revival homes have been a showstopping draw since the days of Old Hollywood. I love their rambling nature and eye-candy embellishments that are too often forgotten in the modern world's typically spare, streamlined spaces. Sometimes Mediterranean-style houses are bi-level, but there is always a connection to the outside and towering palm trees beckoning from the window. They feel as storied and redolent as a Moroccan riad, and every bit as transportive — no passport necessary. These rooms are as good as a magic-carpet ride when it comes to enveloping you in a fantasy and carrying you away to adventures unknown, all within the comforts of home.

Mix it up: high and low, light and dark, solid and patterned. This is what makes rooms really beautiful. Framing modern art pieces, such as this one by William McLure, with symmetrically placed lamps gives the eye a rest. Slightly faded linens impart a leisurely sensibility. A big potted palm brings the outdoors in.

Moroccan bowls echo the colors of the Pacific Ocean down the hallway.

A forged-iron stool delights with its graceful silhouette.

Leafy flora, from ferns to spider plants, has a calming effect in an indoor-outdoor entryway and looks extra lush next to a sleek modern sculpture.

Dark mahogany woodwork throughout the house adds punctuation.

ABOVE: A living room's palette of sandy neutrals, soft salmons, taupes, seafoams, and flax-linen whites is easygoing but never boring; it turns the potted palm trees into an exuberant focal point.
OPPOSITE: Bronze windows and doors act as frames to the indoors and out.

Three islands—two in dark-stained wood, one topped with marble—supply this kitchen with an age-old feel (hanging pots and pans have the same effect). Brass fixtures, pendants from Charles Edwards, and other touches unify the look.

ABOVE: Dark walnut bookcases mirror the dark walnut doors in this living
space, where an antique Italian mantel provides a historic focal point.
OPPOSITE: Unfettered sunlight streams into the breakfast nook each morning.

Antique Italian parquet flooring provides an intricate milieu for equally complex fabric patterns in rich velvets and linens, deep blues, and carved pieces. The ottoman was upholstered in a vintage rug.

Rough-hewn textures—a stone sink, nubby raw linen upholstery, grass-cloth walls—furnish spaces with landmark quality.

White on white on white interiors echo the colorways of Santorini, Greece, and have a serene effect—especially in a bedroom. (Here, the bed floats in the middle of the space, facing the sea.) Woven baskets, pottery, and burnished finishes give a storied sensibility.

Glazed in white, delicate earthenware ceramics will never get old.

A layer of gauzy sheers behind quilted curtains filters daylight to beautiful effect.

A well-loved wooden piece, such as this antique dressing table, can supply warmth in a bathroom.

There are ocean views from the deep soaking tub and fresh sea breezes coming in the open windows.

BEAUTIFUL

LIVING WITH WHAT YOU LOVE

firmly believe that beauty can save the world. It may seem silly with all the negativity in the news cycle, but more beauty—and with it, more love—might be what helps us prevail. That's one reason why making our homes beautiful is so essential. The place you return to for rest and relaxation should be your sanctuary, filled with things you love and enjoy.

Our own 1920s house is Mediterranean in style, with Hollywood Regency details and a traditional layout and footprint. The doors and windows sit open to the gardens, which are lined with boxwoods and a twenty-foot-high ficus hedge. Inside, rooms are stocked with things we've loved for ages: collections of fashion and design magazines that I have stashed since 1998, an 1800s English tilt-top table that's now in the guest bedroom, and a nineteenth-century chinoiserie armoire that was one of our first purchases together.

I found muses for our place in the homes of a few key tastemakers, like the ever refined Bunny Mellon, whose 4,000-acre Virginia estate was the epitome of enchanted, thanks to her lifelong passion for gardening. Then there's Hubert de Givenchy's Le Clos Fiorentina in Cap Ferrat, *(continued on page 235)*

PREVIOUS PAGE: Tidily trimmed boxwoods, a pea-gravel path, and fig ivy-covered walls give our 1928 Hollywood Hills home an added aura of history. OPPOSITE AND ABOVE: Beauty is everywhere! Bringing the outdoors in is vital for human happiness—as evidenced by the parade of lush myrtle topiaries flanking the doors to the garden.

PREVIOUS PAGES: In the living room, the biggest change was the new neoclassical bookshelves. Mixing pieces from various periods—a modernist side table here, a gilded Rococo one there—ensures a curated look. ABOVE: We surround ourselves with things we love, like bountiful collections, including books, blue-and-white porcelain, and shagreen boxes. OPPOSITE: Clustering and stacking boxes supplies artful appeal, as does the mix of African baskets we purchased on safari in South Africa.

France, which was brimming with wicker, loads of slipcovers, and blue-and-white rooms. I'm also inspired by the effortless Caribbean vibe one finds at Bunny Williams and John Rosselli's Punta Cana home, as well as Oscar de la Renta's seafront compound (both in the Dominican Republic). Legendary interiors like theirs aren't born overnight. Michael and I moved into this home ten years ago, and we have redecorated it three times! It's really about how rooms function. Our initial revamp was limited mostly to the kitchen and bathrooms, and we completely overhauled the garden. Since then, most of the furniture has been re-covered and moved around from room to room. But in this newest iteration, we wanted to make it more casual.

A home should evolve as your life changes, and your life *will* change. Michael and I are both different people than we were ten years ago in terms of what we want out of this house and the rooms that we spend time in. The goal is always to live in every room, and now we actually do. Take the redone dining room: we used to never go in, and now we do yoga there. Ultimately, a house needs breathing room. Like a person, it should adapt and grow, becoming more itself with age. You don't have to completely start over with a renovation; it's OK to modify and adjust and rearrange as the years roll on.

And remember, above all, that the definition of *beautiful* is subjective. It doesn't matter what style of home you have, or even what you have. Surround yourself with what you're passionate about and appreciate. True joy comes from following your dreams and finding inspiration around you. If you feel like your home is comfortable and inviting, reflects who you are, and makes you happy, it is beautiful. In fact, because it is yours, it's *more* beautiful.

OPPOSITE: Keeping some of our favorite design tomes within reach means we'll actually read them, a fantastic inspiration boost. Ditto the bar: who doesn't love easy access to an afternoon cocktail? The background fabric is Schumacher's Santa Barbara Ikat in Indigo. FOLLOWING PAGES: The arched French doors in our living room seamlessly lead the way to outdoor living. Trimmed hedges and bounteous boxwoods in terra-cotta pots nod to the centuries-old gardens of Europe.

"I'm going to make every-thing around me beautiful— that will be my life."

Elsie de Wolfe

CLOCKWISE FROM TOP LEFT: Chintz always makes me happy, and you can never have too much. A tray collects finds in one place for a cleaner look. *Beautiful*, my first book, is always top of the stack. Gleaming bar accoutrements add glamour. Ruffles equal easygoing elegance. Hurricanes, antique bowls, and books galore proffer a note of lived-in style, especially as the sunlight pours in.

RIGHT: In the garden, we reupholstered the cushions of the furniture we've had for years in a vibrant new cobalt blue and buttoned-up white piping to add a splash. The hues seem to make the surrounding ficus hedges and topiaries all the more luscious.
FOLLOWING PAGES: A lush ficus and potted ferns on pedestals give nature prime placement and draw the eye up into the space. Bleached and whitewashed wood floors have a breezy quality.

ABOVE: French ticking, blue-and-white checks, Indian block prints, plush Persian blue velvets—when employed together, they're even prettier. OPPOSITE: We dressed nearly every inch of our dining room in a blue-and-white biased gingham by Brunschwig & Fils, a look that is happiness incarnate. A new pair of tufted settees means we use the space much more often than we used to. Italian Bonacina wicker chairs add texture.

RIGHT: Our library, which I tented in a striped fabric I designed for Schumacher, houses a twenty-five-year collection of shelter and fashion magazines. With plenty of comfortable spots to lounge, it's a dreamy place to while away an afternoon; we often pull up chairs to the table to peruse. FOLLOWING PAGES: Function marries form on the tabletop, where the urns house pens, boxes hold Post-its for flagging pages, and candles in hurricane holders can be lit to cast a glow in the evening hours. Leaning framed art pieces against the shelves adds a casual effect to the room.

Blue and white forever!
It is arguably the
most joyful color
pairing—like summer sky
and cumulus clouds—
which is why you'll find
it all over our home.

OPPOSITE: The shell mirror over the chinoiserie commode was designed by Atelier MVM; the chair is Italian wicker. The background fabric is Soane Britain's Fez Stripe in Azure. ABOVE: There's nothing more wonderful than a canopy bed swaddled in flowing fabric panels. It gets all the more welcoming when you add layers of linens—scallop-edged D. Porthault sheets and embroidered blankets alike.

"Have nothing in your home that you do not know to be useful or believe to be beautiful."

— *William Morris*

CLOCKWISE FROM TOP LEFT: A shellwork mirror displays the sea's bounty. A Gracie wallpaper and D. Porthault sheets are a beautiful ode to dreamland. An antique coromandel lacquer screen. Scalloped bullion fringe graces an ottoman with a pieced border. Wide stripes, thin stripes—they all play well together. A trifecta of replica Louis XVI armchairs upholstered in a divine faint blue brushed cotton.

"The power of finding beauty in the humblest things makes home happy and life lovely."

Louisa May Alcott

OPPOSITE: Walking from one chinoiserie-ornamented room to another tented in blue and white stripes is like opening a present. FOLLOWING PAGES: Ceilings are too often forgotten. They're an ideal place for a flurry of embellishments, like my fabric for Schumacher—the same one we used in the library. What's more divine than a tented blue and white-striped room with intricate trims?

"Beauty begins the moment
you decide to be yourself."

Coco Chanel

OPPOSITE: Slipcovering antique chairs (the fabric is my Santa Barbara Ikat for Schumacher)
is a practical yet pretty way to update them for a new era. With twisted cords and
French knots to secure them, they're especially chic. FOLLOWING PAGES: This room is a literal
treasure trove of finds from Carlton Hobbs and James Sansum, including chinoiserie,
a French commode, English antiques, and a plaster table. A painted Gracie wallcovering
along with Vladimir Kanevsky porcelain flowers feels like a luxuriant garden.

ABOVE: I found a muse for the color palette in the extraordinary Parisian *chambre* of Pauline de Rothschild. OPPOSITE: Porcelain flowers by sculptor Vladimir Kanevsky are just as enchanting as the real thing and will never wilt. Keeping a stash of reading material under a nightstand is the homiest possible touch; these showcase some of my favorite things, including *Vogue* back issues and auction catalogs from the estates of Bunny Mellon, Jacqueline Kennedy, and Givenchy. Truly, I'll die with those things sitting beside me!

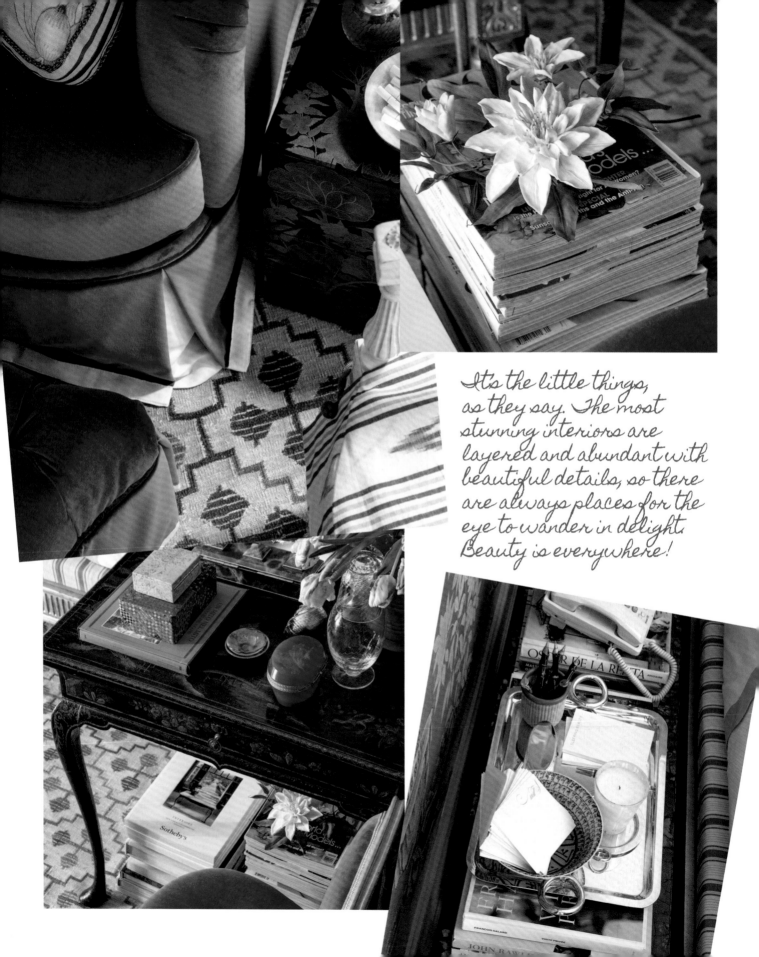

It's the little things,
as they say. The most
stunning interiors are
layered and abundant with
beautiful details, so there
are always places for the
eye to wander in delight.
Beauty is everywhere!

RESOURCES

ARCHITECTS

Appleton Partners LLP Architects
appleton-architects.com

Ferguson & Shamamian Architects
fergusonshamamian.com

James B. Laughlin
jamesblaughlin.com

Walker Warner Architects
walkerwarner.com

Paul Brant Williger
willigerarchitect.com

Winick Architects
winickarchitects.com

ANTIQUES

The Antique and Artisan Gallery
theantiqueandartisangallery.com

Carlton Hobbs *carltonhobbs.com*

Caroline Faison Antiques
daltonbain.com/carolinefaison

Charles Jacobsen
charlesjacobsen.com

Gerald Bland *geraldblandinc.com*

Guinevere *guinevere.co.uk*

James Sansum *jamessansum.com*

JF Chen *jfchen.com*

John Rosselli Antiques
johnrosselliantiques.com

Lief *liefalmont.com*

Loft Antiques and Design
antoniojcrespo.com

Lucca Antiques *luccaantiques.com*

Navona Antiques
navonaantiques.com

Newel *newel.com*

Objets Plus *objetsplus.com*

Parc Monceau *parcmonceauatl.com*

CURTAINS AND CUSTOM UPHOLSTERY

Valley Drapery and Upholstery
valleydrapery.com

DECORATIVE PAINTERS

Bob Christian Decorative Art
bobchristiandecorativeart.com

Mary Meade Evans
marymeadeevans.com

Brian Leaver *brianleaver.com*

Maria Trimbell Murals
mariatrimbell.com

FABRICS

Bennison Fabrics *bennisonfabrics.com*

Brunschwig & Fils *brunschwig.com*

Bujosa *bujosatextil.com*

Carleton V *carletonvltd.com*

Carolina Irving Textiles *www.carolinairvingtextiles.com*

C&C Milano *cec-milano.com*

Chelsea Textiles *chelseatextiles.com*

Claremont *claremontfurnishing.com*

Clarence House *clarencehouse.com*

Classic Cloth *wellstextiles.com*

Colefax and Fowler *colefax.com*

Cowtan & Tout *cowtan.com*

Fermoie *fermoie.com*

Holland & Sherry
hollandandsherry.com

Jane Shelton *janeshelton.com*

Jennifer Shorto *jennifershorto.com*

Katie Ridder *katieridder.com*

Kerry Joyce *kerryjoycetextiles.com*

Lee Jofa *leejofa.com*

Les Indiennes *lesindiennes.com*

Lisa Fine Textiles *lisafinetextiles.com*

Michael S Smith *michaelsmithinc.com*

Muriel Brandolini
murielbrandolini.com

Namay Samay *namaysamay.com*

Penny Morrison *pennymorrison.com*

Peter Dunham Textiles
peterdunhamtextiles.com

Pierre Frey *pierrefrey.com*

Pigott's Store *pigottsstore.com.au*

Quadrille *quadrillefabrics.com*

Raoul Textiles *raoultextiles.com*

Robert Kime *robertkime.com*

Rogers & Goffigon
rogersandgoffigon.com

Rose Tarlow Melrose House
rosetarlow.com

Scalamandré *scalamandre.com*

Schumacher *fschumacher.com*

Schuyler Samperton Textiles
schuylersampertontextiles.com

Sister Parish Design
sisterparishdesign.com

Soane Britain *soane.co.uk*

FURNITURE MAKERS

Aesthetic *aestheticdecor.com*

Atelier MVM *ateliermvm.com*

Bielecky Brothers
bieleckybrothers.com

Bonacina *bonacina1889.it*

Bunny Williams Home
bunnywilliamshome.com

Burden *jonathanburden.com*

Chaddock *chaddockhome.com*

Démiurge *demiurgenyc.com*

Dennis & Leen *dennisandleen.com*

Formations *formationsusa.com*

George Smith *georgesmith.com*

Gregorius Pineo *gregoriuspineo.com*

Hickory Chair *hickorychair.com*

Highland House *highlandhousefurniture.com*

Iatesta Studio *davidiatesta.com*

John Himmel Decorative Arts *johnhimmel.com*

Jonas *jonasworkroom.com*

McKinnon and Harris *mckinnonharris.com*

Munder Skiles *munder-skiles.com*

Oomph *oomphhome.com*

Petersen Antiques *petersenantiques.com*

Rigo's Custom Furniture *rigosfurniture.com*

Rose Tarlow Melrose House *rosetarlow.com*

Soane Britain *soane.co.uk*

The Wicker Works *thewickerworks.com*

GARDEN DESIGN

Cushing Landscape Design *cushinglandscapedesign.com*

Deborah Nevins & Associates *dnalandscape.com*

Denler Hobart Gardens *denlerhobartgardens.com*

LIGHTING

Ann-Morris *annmorrislighting.com*

Charles Edwards *charlesedwards.com*

Christopher Spitzmiller *christopherspitzmiller.com*

Collier Webb *collierwebb.com*

Galerie des Lampes *galeriedeslampes.com*

Hector Finch *hectorfinch.com*

Hudson Valley Lighting *hudsonvalleylighting.com*

Jamb *jamb.co.uk*

Niermann Weeks *niermannweeks.com*

Paul Ferrante *paulferrante.com*

Reborn Antiques *rebornantiques.net*

Rose Tarlow Melrose House *rosetarlow.com*

The Urban Electric Co. *urbanelectric.com*

Vaughan *vaughandesigns.com*

Visual Comfort *visualcomfort.com*

LINENS

Charmajesty *charmajesty.com*

D. Porthault *dporthaultparis.com*

Julia B. *juliab.com*

Leontine Linens *leontinelinens.com*

Matouk *matouk.com*

Pine Cone Hill *annieselke.com*

Walker Valentine *www.walkervalentine.com*

PAINT

Farrow & Ball *farrow-ball.com*

RUGS

Annie Selke *annieselke.com*

Anthony Monaco Carpet & Textile Design *amctdesign.com*

Elizabeth Eakins *elizabetheakins.com*

Guinevere *guinevere.co.uk*

Marc Phillips Decorative Rugs *marcphillipsrugs.com*

Merida *meridastudio.com*

PFM *pattersonflynnmartin.com*

Stark *starkcarpet.com*

Tony Kitz Gallery *tonykitzgallery.com*

SPECIALTY STORES

Amy Berry *amyberryhome.com*

Blue Pheasant *bluepheasant.com*

Bungalow Classic *bungalowclassic.com*

FOUND *foundforthehome.com*

Harbinger *harbingerla.com*

Hollywood at Home *hollywoodathome.com*

Hudson Grace *hudsongracesf.com*

KRB *krbnyc.com*

March *marchsf.com*

Mecox *mecox.com*

Meg Braff *megbraffdesigns.com*

Nickey Kehoe *nickeykehoe.com*

Nicky Rising *nickyrising.com*

Paloma & Co. *shoppalomaandco.com*

Sarah Bartholomew *sarahbartholomew.com/sb/*

Well Made Home *wellmadehome.com*

William Laman *williamlaman.com*

TRIMMINGS

Houlès *houles.com*

Samuel & Sons *samuelandsons.com*

WALLCOVERINGS

Christopher Farr *christopherfarr.com*

De Gournay *degournay.com*

Galbraith & Paul *galbraithandpaul.com*

Gracie *graciestudio.com*

Morris & Co. *stylelibrary.com*

Iksel *iksel.com*

Peter Fasano *peterfasano.com*

Phillip Jeffries *phillipjeffries.com*

ACKNOWLEDGMENTS

It takes a particularly ambitious village to put together a book like this, and I couldn't have done it alone. I must begin by thanking my incredible clients, who share my vision that a beautiful life begins at home. My heartfelt thanks, too, to all the people that come together to create each project we design at Mark D. Sikes Inc.: my amazing partners, including Valley Drapery and Upholstery; our MDS team—you are tenacious and a constant joy to work with; and the many talented collaborators on my collections, including Chaddock (furniture), Soane Britain (rattan furniture), Hudson Valley Lighting, Troy Lighting, Schumacher (fabrics), Merida (rugs), Blue Pheasant (tabletop) and Annie Selke (linens and rugs). To the brilliant team behind this book: photographer Amy Neunsinger, who is as kind as she is talented, agent Jill Cohen, editor Kathleen Jayes, publisher Charles Miers, designers Doug Turshen and Steve Turner, and writer Kathryn O'Shea-Evans—you see the beauty I see and have helped me share it with the world in the loveliest way. Thank you. And finally, to my immediate family and to my better half, Michael: we go together like blue and white. All the beauty in the world is nothing without you—and H.R.H. Lily—to enjoy it with!

First published in the United States of America in 2020 by
Rizzoli International Publications, Inc.
300 Park Avenue South
New York, NY 10010
www.rizzoliusa.com

Copyright © 2020 Mark D. Sikes
Text: Kathryn O'Shea Evans
All images by Amy Neunsinger except:
Pages 30, 32-33 by David Hillegas

Publisher: Charles Miers
Senior Editor: Kathleen Jayes
Design: Doug Turshen with Steve Turner
Production Manager: Kaija Markoe
Managing Editor: Lynn Scrabis

Printed in Italy

2020 2021 2022 2023 / 10 9 8 7 6 5 4 3

ISBN: 978-0-8478-6226-9
Library of Congress Control Number: 2020936693

Visit us online:
Facebook.com/RizzoliNewYork
Twitter: @Rizzoli_Books
Instagram.com/RizzoliBooks
Pinterest.com/RizzoliBooks
Youtube.com/user/RizzoliNY
Issuu.com/Rizzoli